# BASIC BEGINNINGS

*Other Avon Camelot Books by*
**Susan Drake Lipscomb and**
**Margaret Ann Zuanich**

BASIC FUN: COMPUTER GAMES, PUZZLES AND PROBLEMS CHILDREN CAN WRITE

*Coming Soon*

BASIC FUN WITH GRAPHICS: The Apple ® Computer Way
BASIC FUN WITH GRAPHICS: The Atari ® Computer Way
BASIC FUN WITH GRAPHICS: The IBM/PC ® Way

SUSAN DRAKE LIPSCOMB and MARGARET ANN ZUANICH have a unique combination of skills that contributed to the creation of BASIC BEGINNINGS. Susan Lipscomb holds a Master's Degree in Education and has spent fourteen years in the area of language and learning disabilities. Margaret Zuanich's experience in the computer field has included everything from programming to management consulting. She earned her Master's Degree in Business and is now involved in computer systems training. They both live in Palo Alto, California.

# BASIC BEGINNINGS

BY SUSAN DRAKE LIPSCOMB
AND MARGARET ANN ZUANICH

2nd grade reading level has been determined by using the Fry Readability Scale.

BASIC BEGINNINGS is an original publication of Avon Books. This work has never before appeared in book form.

Front cover photograph shows an Apple ® II computer. Apple is a registered trademark of Apple Computer, Inc.

AVON BOOKS
A division of
The Hearst Corporation
959 Eighth Avenue
New York, New York 10019


Published by arrangement with the authors
Library of Congress Catalog Card Number: 83-90621
ISBN: 0-380-83774-9



**Library of Congress Cataloging in Publication Data**

Lipscomb, Susan Drake.
BASIC beginnings.

(An Avon/Camelot book)
Summary: In "play-oriented" approach, explains how to use computers with BASIC programming. Contains notes for parents throughout.
1. Basic (Computer program language)—Juvenile literature. 2. Electronic digital computers—Programming—Juvenile literature. [1. Basic (Computer program language) 2. Programming (Computer)] I. Zuanich, Margaret Ann. II. Title. III. Title: B.A.S.I.C. beginnings.
QA76.73.B3L56 1983 001.64'24 83-90621
ISBN 0-380-83774-9

First Camelot Printing, July, 1983

CAMELOT TRADEMARK REG. U. S. PAT. OFF. AND IN OTHER COUNTRIES, MARCA REGISTRADA, HECHO EN U. S. A.

Printed in the U. S. A.

DON 10 9 8 7 6 5 4 3 2 1

To our children—our constant source
of inspiration and reflection:

Slaton, Paul, Lyn, and Becky

# TABLE OF CONTENTS

# INTRODUCTION

The computer is up and running, and your young child has used the programs and games you've provided. Now you'd like to teach your child simple programming concepts—but how do you get started?

*BASIC Beginnings* gets the two of you under way, using very easy BASIC programs suitable for the child who has begun reading and understands simple arithmetic. You and your child type the programs into the computer and then use a series of Let's Explore activities to experiment with the possibilities of each programming statement. Together, you can expand problem-solving skills and logic as you gain a sense of personal control over the computer.

*BASIC Beginnings* offers an interaction among you, your child and the computer. You can learn right along with your child, and you do not need to be the teacher or the expert.

*BASIC Beginnings* is not a BASIC programming manual. Rather, it is a play-oriented exploration of programming. It teaches what a program is and does, simple BASIC statements, how to RUN and LIST a program, and how to enter data while a program is running. Since *BASIC Beginnings* is intended to broaden the logical thinking skills fundamental to programming, mastery is not the goal—the objectives are exploration, creativity, and self-discovery.

# HINTS FOR PARENTS

Here are some general principles to keep in mind before getting started with *BASIC Beginnings:*

1. Develop an atmosphere of exploration and discovery between you and your child. See yourself as a guide, not a teacher.
2. Work on the computer only when your child is ready and interested in doing so. Use your child's actions and enthusiasm as your guide.
3. Work in short time intervals (fifteen to thirty minutes) as reflected by your child's attention span and motivation. Let his/her responses dictate the level and pace at which you proceed.
4. Be prepared to spend an entire session, or several, elaborating possibilities and explaining the ramifications of only one program.
5. Some children will be content to stay with PRINT programs for a long time, because the PRINT statement is simple enough for most children to create their own programs. Let them.
6. Since each program builds on or expands ideas learned in previous programs, try to use or at least read the programs in order.
7. Encourage your child's creativity at whatever level he/she is successful.
8. Keep in mind that the vocabulary and concepts need only be introduced as seeds. They can be returned to at a later time to be recognized and developed.
9. It is usually best to review and reinforce concepts before introducing new ones. Try to go back and ask some of the more fundamental Let's Explore questions or review previous Parent Notes before launching into the ones accompanying your new program.

10. Don't expect to "take your child through *BASIC Beginnings*" like a course textbook. It is meant to be used, put aside, taken up again, reviewed, and continued throughout the early elementary years.

11. Every computer has a BREAK—or program-interrupt—key. However, some use a different name, or require a combination of keys. Use the programmer's reference manual included with your computer to determine what it uses. In this text we have adopted the convention of referring to this key as the BREAK key.

12. These programs were written in a standard version of BASIC. However, there are a few areas in which computers differ. The Appendix lists the changes necessary to run these programs on certain computers.

# HOW TO USE BASIC BEGINNINGS

1. Type NEW (or SCR for scratch) and press the RETURN key (CR or ENTER) to erase programs currently in memory before you type in each program.

2. Type in the program line by line, including the line numbers, exactly as shown after the word *Program*. Press the RETURN key after each line.

3. Now type RUN and press the RETURN key. The computer will RUN your program. It should look like our RUN.

4. Type LIST and press the RETURN key. The computer will list your original program, ready for you to use in the Let's Explore section.

5. Let's Explore offers questions you can use with your child. The answers follow the questions. When line changes are suggested, type in the changes, type RUN, hit the RETURN key, and see if your RUN matches our example.

6. General programming information and open-ended questions are in Parent Notes. Be sure to read these before you start on a program.

7. To store your programs on tape or disk, there is usually a SAVE command. To retrieve a program, there is a LOAD command. Check your system manual to see what commands are available. Be sure to look at a LIST of the program version currently in memory to be certain it's the particular version you want to save.

# 1 Exploring PRINT
## The Computer Writes

PROGRAMS

1. Riddles
2. Shapes
3. Design
4. Phone List
5. Name and Address
6. Christmas List
7. Initials
8. Spaceship

# RIDDLES

Put your favorite riddle on the computer. Then show your riddle program to your parents or friends. Here is one that we like. Type each line just as it is shown in the program below. Then type RUN and see if your program looks the same as ours.

## PROGRAM

```
100 PRINT "WHAT GETS WETTER AND WETTER"
110 PRINT "THE MORE IT DRIES?"
120 PRINT
130 PRINT
140 PRINT
150 PRINT "A TOWEL!!!"
```

## RUN

```
WHAT GETS WETTER AND WETTER
THE MORE IT DRIES?

A TOWEL!!!
```

## *LET'S EXPLORE*

1. *Now try another riddle. Here is one you can use. Type in the lines shown below, then RUN your program and see if it looks like our RUN.*

```
100 PRINT "WHAT IS BLACK AND WHITE"
110 PRINT "AND RED ALL OVER?"
150 PRINT "AN EMBARRASSED ZEBRA!!!!"
```

RUN

```
WHAT IS BLACK AND WHITE
AND RED ALL OVER?

AN EMBARRASSED ZEBRA!!!!
```

## *PARENT NOTES*

1. The PRINT statement tells the computer to print every character between the quotation marks on your screen or printer.
2. The PRINT statements on lines 120, 130, and 140 each print a blank line.
3. To change an existing line in a program, retype the line using the same line number.

# SHAPES

Use the computer to draw shapes. Type this program into your computer and you can make a square.

PROGRAM

```
100 PRINT "*******"
110 PRINT "*     *"
120 PRINT "*     *"
130 PRINT "*     *"
140 PRINT "*******"
```

RUN

```
*******
*     *
*     *
*     *
*******
```

*LET'S EXPLORE*

1. *How would you change this program to make a rectangle?*

   *Delete lines 120 and 130 by typing:*

```
120
130
```

RUN

```
*******
*     *
*******
```

*2. Now, can you make a triangle?*

```
100 PRINT "* * * *"
110 PRINT " *   *"
120 PRINT "  * *"
130 PRINT "   *"
140
```

RUN

```
* * * *
 *   *
  * *
   *
```

## *PARENT NOTES*

1. In order to delete a line in a program, just type the line number and hit RETURN.
2. Once your child has tried these shapes, suggest other ones, such as a circle or trapezoid.

# DESIGN

Here is a design we made with our computer. Try it on yours.

PROGRAM

```
100 PRINT "**************"
110 PRINT "*****(())*****"
120 PRINT "***(((())))***"
130 PRINT "*(((((())))))*"
140 PRINT "***(((())))***"
150 PRINT "*****(())*****"
160 PRINT "**************"
```

RUN

```
**************
*****(())*****
***(((())))***
*(((((())))))*
***(((())))***
*****(())*****
**************
```

## *LET'S EXPLORE*

1. *It is easy to change this design. Make these changes and see what happens:*

```
100 PRINT "  **********"
160 PRINT "  **********"
```

RUN

```
  **********
*****(())*****
***(((())))***
*(((((())))))*
***(((())))***
*****(())*****
  **********
```

## *PARENT NOTES*

1. Encourage your child to make up an original design using many of the special characters on the keyboard of your computer.

# PHONE LIST

Put your favorite friends' phone numbers on your computer. Then you can always find the phone number when you want to call. Just type in their names and numbers instead of ours between the quotation marks in the program.

## PROGRAM

```
100 PRINT "SLATON       493-1233"
110 PRINT "MARK         941-5521"
120 PRINT "BILL         494-2945"
130 PRINT "JOHN         941-4434"
```

## RUN

```
SLATON      493-1233
MARK        941-5521
BILL        494-2945
JOHN        941-4434
```

## *LET'S EXPLORE*

1. *If one of your friends changes his number, how can you correct it on your list?*

   `Retype the line.`

2. *If someone moves away, how can you erase him from your list?*

   `Type the Line number and hit RETURN.`

3. *How can you add new friends to your list?*

   `Add Line numbers to your program.`

## *PARENT NOTES*

1. To add more lines to a program, use line numbers larger than the last ones in the program.

# NAME AND ADDRESS

The computer can print your name and address. Just replace the name and address in this program with your own.

PROGRAM

```
100 PRINT "JOE BLOE"
110 PRINT "43 FIRST STREET"
120 PRINT "SILVER CITY, CA 94306"
```

RUN

```
JOE BLOE
43 FIRST STREET
SILVER CITY, CA 94306
```

*LET'S EXPLORE*

1. *Type in this line and see what happens:*

   *105 PRINT*

```
105 PRINT
```

RUN

```
JOE BLOE

43 FIRST STREET
SILVER CITY, CA 94306
```

2. *To add friends to your list, add more line numbers to the end of your original program.*

```
105
130 PRINT
140 PRINT "JOHN DOE"
150 PRINT "6 OAK ROAD"
160 PRINT "MIAMI, FL 33133"
```

RUN

```
JOE BLOE
43 FIRST STREET
SILVER CITY, CA 94306

JOHN DOE
6 OAK ROAD
MIAMI, FL 33133
```

## *PARENT NOTES*

1. Ask your child what happens if you forget one of the pairs of quotation marks in a PRINT statement. (Results vary according to computer. Experiment.)

# CHRISTMAS LIST

Christmas isn't far away, and your parents need a list of the gifts you want. Use your computer to write your list. Just put the presents you want into this program. It's easy to add to your list later.

## PROGRAM

```
100 PRINT "CAMERA"
110 PRINT "DIRT BIKE"
120 PRINT "TAPE RECORDER"
130 PRINT "DOG"
140 PRINT "COMPUTER"
150 PRINT "GAMES"
```

## RUN

```
CAMERA
DIRT BIKE
TAPE RECORDER
DOG
COMPUTER
GAMES
```

## *LET'S EXPLORE*

1. *Use this same program to make a list of goodies you want your mom to buy at the grocery store.*

```
100 PRINT "M&M's"
110 PRINT "GRAPE JUICE"
120 PRINT "ROCKY ROAD ICE CREAM"
130 PRINT "CHIPS"
140 PRINT "RASPBERRY YOGURT"
150 PRINT "BAGELS"
```

RUN

```
M&M's
ORAPE JIITCE
ROCKY ROAD ICE CREAM
CHIPS
RASPBERRY YOGURT
BAGELS
```

## *PARENT NOTES*

1. The cursor is a moving or blinking symbol on the screen which indicates where the next character will appear. Use this program to experiment with the edit features of your computer. Help your child:
   —backspace and erase
   —move the cursor to a particular location in a line without erasing.
   Remember to press the RETURN or ENTER key after each correction.
2. Help him/her:
   —delete a line or character
   —insert a line or character.
3. Encourage him/her to get a new LIST after each change to be certain it was entered correctly.

# INITIALS

Draw large letters on the screen using the initials of your name.

## PROGRAM

```
100 PRINT "        J     SSSSSSS"
110 PRINT "        J   SSS"
120 PRINT "        J     SSSSSS"
130 PRINT "J       J         SSS"
140 PRINT " JJJJJJ     SSSSSSS"
```

## RUN

```
        J     SSSSSSS
        J   SSS
        J     SSSSSS
J       J         SSS
 JJJJJJ     SSSSSSS
```

## *LET'S EXPLORE*

1. *Try making up a brand for yourself using your own initials. Draw a copy of your brand on a piece of graph paper. Then count out the lines and spaces you need.*

```
100 PRINT "L"
110 PRINT "L"
120 PRINT "L  L"
130 PRINT "L  L"
140 PRINT "LLLLLL"
150 PRINT "   L"
160 PRINT "   LLLLLL"
```

RUN

```
L
L
L    L
L    L
LLLLLL
     L
     LLLLLL
```

## *PARENT NOTES*

1. Most computers display 40 columns across and 20 to 30 lines down. Your owner's manual will give you the exact number for your computer.

# SPACESHIP

Try making a drawing with the computer. Here is one of a spaceship.

## PROGRAM

```
100 PRINT
110 PRINT "          ^"
120 PRINT "         / \"
130 PRINT "        /   \"
140 PRINT "       /     \"
150 PRINT "      /       \"
160 PRINT "     /         \"
170 PRINT "     I         I"
180 PRINT "     I         I"
190 PRINT "     I    U    I"
200 PRINT "     I         I"
210 PRINT "     I    S    I"
220 PRINT "     I         I"
230 PRINT "     I    A    I"
240 PRINT "     I         I"
250 PRINT "     I         I"
260 PRINT "    /           \"
270 PRINT "   /             \"
280 PRINT "  /               \"
290 PRINT " /                 \"
300 PRINT "/===================\"
```

RUN

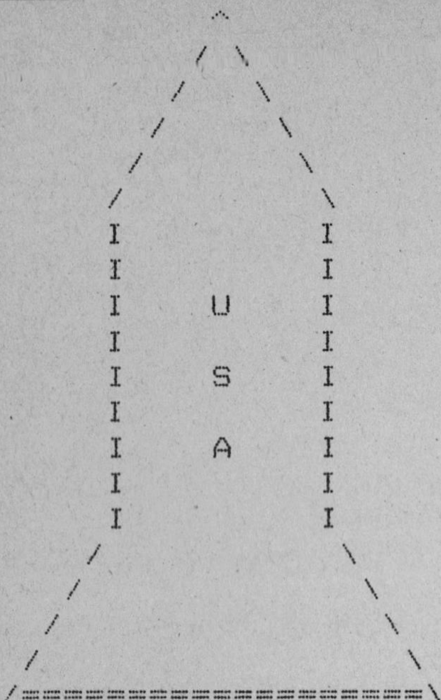

## *LET'S EXPLORE*

*1. Make up a spaceship of your own, a face or a jet plane, or try making this house.*

```
100 PRINT "   /\\\\\\\\\\\\\\\"
110 PRINT "  /   \\\\\\\\\\\\\\"
120 PRINT " /      \\\\\\\\\\\\\"
130 PRINT "/  _   _  \\\\\\\\\\\\"
140 PRINT "I I_I I_I I          I"
150 PRINT "I         I   __     I"
160 PRINT "I    _    I  I__I    I"
170 PRINT "I   I I   I          I"
180 PRINT "I___I I___I__________I"
```

RUN

```
   /\\\\\\\\\\\\\\\
  /   \\\\\\\\\\\\\\
 /      \\\\\\\\\\\\\
/  _   _  \\\\\\\\\\\\
I I_I I_I I          I
I         I   __     I
I    _    I  I__I    I
I   I I   I          I
I___I I___I__________I
```

## *PARENT NOTES*

1. Don't forget to clear out the work space by typing NEW or SCR before you start on the house.
2. Encourage your child to use the unique keys and characters of your computer.
3. Help your child use graph paper to design his picture, if it makes the task easier for him.

# 2 Exploring LET
## Math Wizard

## PROGRAMS

1. Calculator
2. Money
3. Book Club
4. Sales Tax

# CALCULATOR

It's easy to use your computer for arithmetic. This program tells you the answer to 2 + 4.

PROGRAM

```
100 PRINT 2+4
```

RUN

```
 6
```

*LET'S EXPLORE*

1. *Now change your program to add 15 + 10.*

```
100 PRINT 15+10
```

RUN

```
 25
```

2. *If you want to tell the computer to subtract, use the minus sign. This program gives the answer to 20 − 5.*

```
100 PRINT 20-5
```

RUN

```
 15
```

3. *To multiply on the computer, use the * (asterisk). Change your program to multiply 3 times 3.*

```
100 PRINT 3*3
```

RUN

```
 9
```

4. *Tell the computer to divide by using the / (slash). This program divides 50 by 10.*

```
100 PRINT 50/10
```

RUN

```
 5
```

## *PARENT NOTES*

1. Encourage your child to think up other numbers to use in these operations.
2. Help him/her invent simple problems, such as how many pets in your household, the total number of cousins, etc. Then use this program to get the answer.
3. Warning! If your child uses very large or very small numbers, the results could be printed out in scientific notation, i.e. 1.057E03. To translate this number from scientific notation, move the decimal point 3 places to the right. 1.057E03 becomes 1057. If the letter E is followed by a minus sign, the decimal point is moved to the left. 1.057E-3 becomes .00157
4. If your child uses extremely large numbers, you could get an OVERFLOW WARNING. This means you are trying to do a calculation with a number too large for your computer.

# MONEY

I have a penny, a nickel, and a quarter. This program tells me how much money I have altogether.

PROGRAM

```
100 LET X=.01
110 LET Y=.05
120 LET Z=.25
130 LET T=X+Y+Z
140 PRINT T
```

RUN

```
 .31
```

*LET'S EXPLORE*

1. *If you earned another nickel, can you change this program so it tells you how much money you have now?*

```
125 LET A=.05
130 LET T=X+Y+Z+A
```

RUN

```
 .36
```

2. *If you spent the quarter, how can you change the program?*

```
120
130 LET T=X+Y+A
```

RUN

```
.11
```

3. *Now make up your own numbers and put them in this program.*

## *PARENT NOTES*

1. T, X, Y, A, and Z are called *numeric variables*. They are names of locations in the computer's memory used to store numbers for calculations. You can use any of the letters from A to Z for *numeric variables*.
2. The LET statement assigns the value on the right side of the equal sign to the numeric variable on the left side of the equal sign.
3. When your child uses numbers other than the ones shown, your computer may not print the final zeros after a decimal point (i.e., instead of .40 you may see .4).
4. Encourage your child to solve a practical problem using this type of program. For instance, find out how much money is in a handful of coins, etc.

# BOOK CLUB

We want to order 2 books from the school book club. One book costs $.52 and the other $.75. This program shows how much money we need.

PROGRAM

```
100 LET X=.52
110 LET Y=.75
120 LET T=X+Y
130 PRINT "YOUR BOOKS COST $ ";
140 PRINT T
```

RUN

```
YOUR BOOKS COST $  1.27
```

*LET'S EXPLORE*

1. *If one of the books costs $1.50 instead of $.52, what change should be made to the program?*

```
100 LET X=1.50
```

RUN

```
YOUR BOOKS COST $  2.25
```

2. *If we want to buy a third book which costs $.48, what changes need to be made?*

```
115 LET Z=.48
120 LET T=X+Y+Z
```

RUN

```
YOUR BOOKS COST $  2.73
```

*3. Now use some prices of your own in this program.*

## *PARENT NOTES*

1. This program can be used to show the total cost of toys, treats at the store, etc.

# SALES TAX

You're saving for a $5.50 board game and you want to find out how much money you need for sales tax. This program gives you the answer.

## PROGRAM

```
100 LET X=5.50
110 LET Y=.06
120 LET T=X*Y
130 PRINT T
```

## RUN

```
 .33
```

## *LET'S EXPLORE*

1. *If you want to buy a soccer ball that costs $11.00, how would you change this program?*

```
100 LET X=11.00
```

## RUN

```
 .66
```

2. *This program uses a sales tax of 6 percent. Your sales tax might be different. Can you change the program so it uses a sales tax of 4 percent?*

```
110 LET Y=.04
```

## RUN

```
 .44
```

3. *Can you change the program to print out the total amount of money needed?*

```
120 LET T=X+X*Y
```

RUN

```
 11.44
```

4. *Now think of something else you might want to buy, and try changing this program to give you the total cost.*

## *PARENT NOTES*

1. Your child might get answers with more than two decimal places (i.e., 10.754), depending on the tax rate you use. If this occurs, just suggest that he/she ignore all but the first two numbers to the right of the decimal (Change 10.754 to 10.75).

# 3 Exploring GOTO

## Changing the Computer's Path

## PROGRAMS

1. I.D.
2. Counting
3. Fancy Adding
4. Scrambled Message

# I.D.

This program prints a name until you hit the BREAK key.

## PROGRAM

```
100 PRINT "SLATON",
110 GOTO 100
```

## RUN

```
SLATON              SLATON              SLATON
   SLATON           SLATON              SLATON
   SLATON           SLATON              SLATON
   SLATON           SLATON              SLATON
   SLATON           SLATON              SLATON
   SLATON           SLATON              SLATON
   SLATON           SLATON              SLATON
```

## *LET'S EXPLORE*

1. *Make a different pattern with this name by replacing the , (comma) with a ; (semicolon).*

```
100 PRINT "SLATON";
```

## RUN

```
SLATONSLATONSLATONSLATONSLATONSLATON
SLATONSLATONSLATONSLATONSLATONSLATON
SLATONSLATONSLATONSLATONSLATONSLATON
SLATONSLATONSLATONSLATONSLATONSLATON
SLATONSLATONSLATONSLATONSLATONSLATON
SLATONSLATONSLATONSLATONSLATONSLATON
SLATONSLATONSLATONSLATONSLATONSLATON
```

2. *Now take the ; (semicolon) out and see what happens.*

```
100 PRINT "SLATON"
```

RUN

```
SLATON
SLATON
SLATON
SLATON
SLATON
SLATON
SLATON
```

3. *Put your own name or a design between the quotation marks and see what the computer prints out.*

## *PARENT NOTES*

1. This program will continue to run until you hit the BREAK or program-interrupt key. So, before you run this program, show your child how to use this key on your computer.
2. The GOTO statement in Line 110 tells the computer to execute Line 100 again. Rather than explaining this to your child, see if he/she can guess the purpose of Line 110.
3. The number of spaces following a , (comma) and a ; (semicolon) varies among computers. Therefore, your program may not look exactly like this one.

# COUNTING

The computer is very good at counting! This program tells it to count by 2's until you hit the BREAK key.

## PROGRAM

```
100 LET T=0
110 LET T=T+2
120 PRINT T
130 GOTO 110
```

## RUN

```
 2
 4
 6
 8
 10
 12
```

## *LET'S EXPLORE*

1. *If you want the computer to count by 5's, what change would you make?*

```
110 LET T=T+5
```

## RUN

```
 5
 10
 15
 20
 25
 30
```

2. *Can you make the computer count by 10's?*

```
110 LET T=T+10
```

RUN

```
 10
 20
 30
 40
 50
 60
```

3. *What changes would you make if you want the computer to count backwards by 1's from 99?*

```
100 LET T=100
110 LET T=T-1
```

RUN

```
 99
 98
 97
 96
 95
 94
```

4. *Now use some numbers of your own in this program.*

## *PARENT NOTES*

1. Help your child follow the path of the program. Remember the computer executes each line in sequence unless the GOTO statement changes the order.
2. Line 100 gives a starting value to T. See if your child can figure this out.

# FANCY ADDING

The computer does a great job adding numbers together. This program starts with 2 + 2 and keeps going until you hit the BREAK key.

## PROGRAM

```
100 LET X=2
110 LET Y=X+X
120 PRINT X;" + ";X;" = ";Y
130 LET X=X+1
140 GOTO 110
```

## RUN

```
 2  +  2  =  4
 3  +  3  =  6
 4  +  4  =  8
 5  +  5  =  10
 6  +  6  =  12
 7  +  7  =  14
 8  +  8  =  16
```

## *LET'S EXPLORE*

*1. Can you change the program to start with 10 + 10?*

```
100 LET X=10
```

## RUN

```
 10  +  10  =  20
 11  +  11  =  22
 12  +  12  =  24
 13  +  13  =  26
```

```
14   +   14   =   28
15   +   15   =   30
16   +   16   =   32
```

2. *What must you change if you want the computer to multiply instead of add?*

```
110 LET Y=X*X
120 PRINT X;" * ";X;" = ";Y
```

<u>RUN</u>

```
10   *   10   =   100
11   *   11   =   121
12   *   12   =   144
13   *   13   =   169
14   *   14   =   196
15   *   15   =   225
16   *   16   =   256
```

## *PARENT NOTES*

1. The PRINT statement in Line 120 uses both numeric variables—such as X and Y—and characters between " " (quotation marks)—such as " + ". Variables must be separated from quotation marks by either a , (comma) or a ; (semicolon).
2. See if your child can figure out what the program would print if Line 140 said GOTO 100.

# SCRAMBLED MESSAGE

This program prints a message. Can you follow the program and figure out what it says?

## PROGRAM

```
100 GOTO 170
110 PRINT " YOU";
120 GOTO 150
130 PRINT " ARE";
140 GOTO 110
150 PRINT " TODAY?"
160 END
170 PRINT "HI!";
180 GOTO 190
190 PRINT " HOW";
200 GOTO 130
```

## RUN

```
HI! HOW ARE YOU TODAY?
```

## *LET'S EXPLORE*

1. *Can you change two lines to make the program print:*

   *HI! HOW WAS SCHOOL TODAY?*

```
110 PRINT " SCHOOL";
130 PRINT " WAS";
```

## RUN

```
HI! HOW WAS SCHOOL TODAY?
```

2. *Can you write a message of your own?*

## *PARENT NOTES*

1. Try using a three-word message for your child's first original scrambled message.
2. The END statement in Line 160 tells the program to stop at that line. It is used when you want a program to end at a line other than the last one in the program.

# 4 Exploring INPUT
## Using Your Numbers

## PROGRAMS

1. A Car Trip
2. Age
3. Babysit
4. Backpack
5. Conversion

# A CAR TRIP

How long will it take to drive to your cousin's house? Use your computer to find out. Ask your parents how fast they drive and how many miles you will travel. Type in these numbers when the program asks for them. Then you can tell your parents how long the trip will take.

## PROGRAM

```
100 PRINT "MILES"
110 INPUT M
120 PRINT "SPEED"
130 INPUT S
140 LET T=M/S
150 PRINT "HOURS: ";T
```

## RUN

```
MILES
? 350
SPEED
? 50
HOURS:   7
```

## *LET'S EXPLORE*

1. *Now think of a trip you would like to take and let this program give you the answer.*
2. *You can use this same program to find out how long it would take to drive across the U.S., fly around the world, or even go to the moon!*
3. *What happens if you put a ; (semicolon) at the end of the first two PRINT statements?*

```
100 PRINT "MILES";
120 PRINT "SPEED";
```

RUN

```
MILES? 350
SPEED? 50
HOURS:   7
```

4. *When the computer is waiting for a number or an answer from you, it prints a ? (question mark).*

## PARENT NOTES

1. The INPUT statements in Lines 110 and 130 allow you to give the computer different values for miles and speed each time you run the program.
2. Encourage your child to explore different uses for this program. Hint: (1) The circumference of the earth is 25,000 miles. (2) The distance to the moon is 253,000 miles.
3. Help your child replace the LET statements in earlier programs, such as Money and Sales Tax, with INPUT statements.

# AGE

How old was your mother when you were born? Type in your age and your mother's age now. Then this program will tell you.

## PROGRAM

```
100 PRINT "YOUR AGE";
110 INPUT Y
120 PRINT "MOTHER'S AGE";
130 INPUT M
140 LET N=M-Y
150 PRINT "YOUR MOTHER WAS ";N
```

## RUN

```
YOUR AGE? 7
MOTHER'S AGE? 37
YOUR MOTHER WAS  30
```

## *LET'S EXPLORE*

1. *What should you change if you want to use this program for your dad?*

```
120 PRINT "DAD'S AGE";
150 PRINT "YOUR DAD WAS ";N
```

## RUN

```
YOUR AGE? 7
DAD'S AGE? 40
YOUR DAD WAS  33
```

2. *Can you fix this program so it will go back to the beginning and run again?*

```
160 GOTO 100
```

RUN

```
YOUR AGE? 7
DAD'S AGE? 40
YOUR DAD WAS  33
YOUR AGE?
```

## *PARENT NOTES*

1. If your child changes the program to repeat, then you must hit the BREAK key to stop it.
2. The equation in Line 140 works as long as M is greater than Y. To calculate an age difference if Y is greater than M use: 140 LET N = Y − M

# BABYSIT

You want to save up for a $10 board game. Your mom says she will pay a quarter every time you watch your sister for her. How many times will you have to babysit? Just type in the cost of the game, and this program will give you the answer.

PROGRAM

```
100 LET X=.25
110 PRINT "COST";
120 INPUT C
130 LET T=C/X
140 PRINT "YOU MUST BABYSIT ";T;" TIMES"
```

RUN

```
COST? 10.00
YOU MUST BABYSIT  40  TIMES
```

## *LET'S EXPLORE*

1. *You can use this program to help you save for something else too. Just run the program with the cost of what you want.*
2. *If your mom gives you a raise to $.50, how would you change the program?*

```
100 LET X=.50
```

RUN

```
COST? 10.00
YOU MUST BABYSIT  20  TIMES
```

## *PARENT NOTES*

1. Remind your child that the / (slash) in Line 130 tells the computer to divide.
2. Depending on the values you use, this program may print a decimal number for the answer. Just have your child ignore the numbers after the decimal point.

# BACKPACK

You are going on a hiking trip with your parents. They want to know how far the family will travel. Use your computer to figure out the distance. When you run this program, type in the number of days you will hike. The program tells you how many miles you will have hiked at a rate of 5 miles a day by the end of your trip.

## PROGRAM

```
100 LET N=5
110 PRINT "DAYS";
120 INPUT D
130 LET M=N*D
140 PRINT "AT A RATE OF ";N;" MILES
    PER DAY"
150 PRINT "YOU CAN HIKE ";M;" MILES"
160 PRINT "IN ";D;" DAYS"
170 GOTO 100
```

## RUN

```
DAYS? 3
AT A RATE OF  5  MILES PER DAY
YOU CAN HIKE  15  MILES
IN  3  DAYS
DAYS?
```

## *LET'S EXPLORE*

1. *If your family can hike 8 miles in a day, what change must you make to this program?*

```
100 LET N=8
```

RUN

```
DAYS? 3
AT A RATE OF  8  MILES PER DAY
YOU CAN HIKE  24  MILES
IN  3  DAYS
DAYS?
```

2. *Can you change this program so you can input your hiking rate?*

```
100 PRINT "RATE";
105 INPUT N
```

RUN

```
RATE? 10
DAYS? 3
AT A RATE OF  10  MILES PER DAY
YOU CAN HIKE  30  MILES
IN  3  DAYS
RATE?
```

3. *This program repeats so you can run it over and over with different values. To stop it, hit the BREAK key.*

## *PARENT NOTES*

1. Help your child use this program for other trips, such as a bike or car trip.

# CONVERSION

If there are 12 eggs in a dozen, how many eggs are there in 4 dozen? Use the computer to find out. Just run this program and type in the number 4 after the program asks NUMBER OF DOZEN?

## PROGRAM

```
100 PRINT "NUMBER OF DOZEN";
110 INPUT N
120 LET C=12
130 LET T=N*C
140 PRINT "THERE ARE ";T
```

## RUN

```
NUMBER OF DOZEN? 4
THERE ARE  48
```

## *LET'S EXPLORE*

1. *If you have 2 dozen pencils, could you use this program to get the total number of pencils?*

## RUN

```
NUMBER OF DOZEN? 2
THERE ARE  24
```

2. *Change this same program to tell you the total number of inches in 6 feet.*

```
100 PRINT "NUMBER OF FEET";
```

RUN

```
NUMBER OF FEET? 6
THERE ARE  72
```

3. *Now try changing the program to calculate the total number of hours in 4 days.*

```
100 PRINT "NUMBER OF DAYS";
120 LET C=24
```

RUN

```
NUMBER OF DAYS? 4
THERE ARE  96
```

4. *Can you change this program to calculate the number of hours in a week? A month? A year?*

## *PARENT NOTES*

1. Line 120 uses the variable C as the conversion factor. In the first problem C is equal to 12 units in a dozen. To convert hours to days, C is set to 24.
2. Use this program to help your child explore other relationships, such as inches in yards, feet in miles, pounds in tons, etc.

# 5 Exploring Strings

## The Computer Uses Words

# PROGRAMS

1. Mad Poems
2. Mad Sentences
3. Scrambled Story

# MAD POEMS

Now you and the computer can write a short poem. You type in the words that rhyme and the computer types out the poem.

## PROGRAM

```
100 DIM A$(25),B$(25),C$(25)
110 PRINT "NAME";
120 INPUT A$
130 PRINT "TWO RHYMING WORDS";
140 INPUT B$,C$
150 PRINT
160 PRINT A$;" WENT TO THE ";B$
170 PRINT "AND SAW A ";C$
```

## RUN

```
NAME? LUCY FIN
TWO RHYMING WORDS? LAKE,CAKE
LUCY FIN WENT TO THE LAKE
AND SAW A CAKE
```

## *LET'S EXPLORE*

1. *Now RUN the program and use your own rhyming words.*
2. *Can you change the poem in the program so the second line says FOUND instead of SAW?*

```
170 PRINT "AND FOUND A ";C$
```

## RUN

```
NAME? JIM BROWN
TWO RHYMING WORDS? SHORE,DOOR
```

```
JIM BROWN WENT TO THE SHORE
AND FOUND A DOOR
```

3. *Try writing your own poem for this program.*

## *PARENT NOTES*

1. Line 100: The variables A$, B$, C$ are called *string variables.* They are used to store letters and words. The DIM (dimension) statement saves spaces for the letters in a string variable. In this case, each variable can hold 25 letters.
2. Help your child make up other poems to use in this program. If you need more than 2 lines, just use line numbers larger than 170.

# MAD SENTENCES

Your computer can help you make up crazy sentences. When the program asks for them, type in 2 nouns and a verb and see what you come up with.

## PROGRAM

```
100 DIM A$(25),B$(25),C$(25)
110 PRINT "NOUN";
120 INPUT A$
130 PRINT "ANOTHER NOUN";
140 INPUT B$
150 PRINT "VERB";
160 INPUT C$
170 PRINT
180 PRINT "THE TALL ";A$;" AND THE GREEN"
190 PRINT B$;" ";C$;" THE PURPLE MONSTER."
```

## RUN

```
NOUN? MAN
ANOTHER NOUN? ALIEN
VERB? CAUGHT

THE TALL MAN AND THE GREEN
ALIEN CAUGHT THE PURPLE MONSTER.
```

## *LET'S EXPLORE*

1. *Try running the program using your own words.*
2. *Can you change part of the sentence in the program? Suppose you want the monster to be ORANGE instead of PURPLE?*

```
190 PRINT B$;" ";C$;" THE ORANGE MONSTER."
```

RUN

```
NOUN? GIANT
ANOTHER NOUN? LION
VERB? CHASED

THE TALL GIANT AND THE GREEN
LION CHASED THE ORANGE MONSTER.
```

3. *You can make up your own sentences for this program. Just change the words inside the " (quotation marks) in Lines 180 and 190.*

## *PARENT NOTES*

1. String variables can be used in INPUT, LET, and PRINT statements. You can use any letter A-Z followed by a $ (dollar sign) for a string variable, i.e., A$, D$, M$.
2. If you want to put more than 25 letters in these string variables you must change the 25 in the DIM statement to the number of spaces you require.

# SCRAMBLED STORY

Make up your own story about a monster and some of your friends. You can decide who to put into the story and how big your monster is each time you run the program.

## PROGRAM

```
100 DIM C$(25),S$(25),N$(25),M$(25)
110 PRINT "COLOR";
120 INPUT C$
130 PRINT "SIZE";
140 INPUT S$
150 PRINT "NAME";
160 INPUT N$
170 PRINT "ANOTHER NAME";
180 INPUT M$
190 PRINT
200 PRINT "THE ";S$;" MONSTER WITH
    ";C$;" EYES"
210 PRINT "CHASED ";N$;" THROUGH THE WOODS"
220 PRINT "WHILE ";M$;" RAN FOR HELP."
```

## RUN

```
COLOR? ORANGE
SIZE? HUGE
NAME? LUKE SKYWALKER
ANOTHER NAME? PRINCESS LEAH

THE HUGE MONSTER WITH ORANGE EYES
CHASED LUKE SKYWALKER THROUGH THE WOODS
WHILE PRINCESS LEAH RAN FOR HELP.
```

## *LET'S EXPLORE*

1. *You can run this program using your name or the names of your friends.*
2. *You can change the story just by changing a few words in Lines 200, 210, and 220.*
3. *How would you change the program to INPUT another part of the story, such as the verb CHASED?*

```
105 DIM V$(25)
185 PRINT "VERB";
186 INPUT V$
210 PRINT V$;" ";N$;" THROUGH THE WOODS"
```

RUN

```
COLOR? ORANGE
SIZE? HUGE
NAME? LUKE SKYWALKER
ANOTHER NAME? PRINCESS LEAH
VERB? CARRIED

THE HUGE MONSTER WITH ORANGE EYES
CARRIED LUKE SKYWALKER THROUGH THE WOODS
WHILE PRINCESS LEAH RAN FOR HELP.
```

## *PARENT NOTES*

1. Encourage your child to try an original story using this format. To add interest, you can input noun phrases and verb phrases too.

# 6 Exploring More Advanced Programs

## Off and Running

## PROGRAMS

1. More Easy Counting
2. Blast Off
3. Times Tables
4. Stars
5. Shooting Gallery

# MORE EASY COUNTING

This program uses an easy shortcut to help the computer count to 10. It stops by itself when it is finished.

PROGRAM

```
100 FOR N=1 TO 10
110 PRINT N;
120 NEXT N
```

RUN

```
1  2  3  4  5  6  7  8  9  10
```

*LET'S EXPLORE*

1. *If you want to count to 5, change Line 100 like this:*

```
100 FOR N=1 TO 5
```

RUN

```
1  2  3  4  5
```

2. *What would you change if you want to count to 8?*

```
100 FOR N=1 TO 8
```

RUN

```
1  2  3  4  5  6  7  8
```

3. *If you want the computer to count to 40 by 5's, make this change to Line 100.*

```
100 FOR N=5 TO 40 STEP 5
```

RUN

```
5  10  15  20  25  30  35  40
```

4. *Now try some numbers of your own.*

## *PARENT NOTES*

1. Lines 100 and 120 are called a FOR . . . NEXT loop. The computer executes Lines 100, 110 and 120 and then goes back to Line 100 and starts over. Each time Line 100 is executed, the variable N is increased by 1. When N is greater than 10, the program stops.
2. Help your child experiment with this statement by changing the numbers used in Line 100.

# BLAST OFF

You are ready for rocket launch and the computer is ready with the countdown. Just run this program to start the countdown.

PROGRAM

```
100 FOR I=10 TO 1 STEP -1
110 PRINT I
120 NEXT I
130 PRINT "BLAST OFF!"
```

RUN

```
 10
 9
 8
 7
 6
 5
 4
 3
 2
 1
BLAST OFF!
```

*LET'S EXPLORE*

1. *This is another FOR . . . NEXT loop, only this one counts backwards. Notice that Line 100 has STEP −1. The −1 makes the computer count backwards. Try changing the program so it counts backwards by 10 starting with 100.*

```
100 FOR I=100 TO 10 STEP -10
```

RUN

```
 100
 90
 80
 70
 60
 50
 40
 30
 20
 10
BLAST OFF!
```

## *PARENT NOTES*

1. The FOR . . . NEXT loop can also be used to count backwards. In this case, STEP −1 tells the computer to subtract 1 from the starting value until the ending value is reached.
2. Help your child expand this program by adding other PRINT statements within the FOR . . . NEXT loop, or after the NEXT statement.

# TIMES TABLES

Practice your multiplication tables with your computer. This program asks you for the number you want to use and then checks your answer on that number times 1 through 10. See how fast you can do your tables!

## PROGRAM

```
100 PRINT "NUMBER";
110 INPUT N
120 FOR I=1 TO 10
130 PRINT N;" * ";I;" = ";
140 INPUT M
150 IF M=N*I THEN 180
160 PRINT "SORRY -- TRY AGAIN"
170 GOTO 130
180 PRINT "GREAT!!"
190 NEXT I
```

## RUN

```
NUMBER? 5
 5  *  1  = ? 5
GREAT!!
 5  *  2  = ? 10
GREAT!!
 5  *  3  = ? 20
SORRY -- TRY AGAIN
 5  *  3  = ? 15
GREAT!!
 5  *  4  = ?
```

## *LET'S EXPLORE*

1. *Can you change this program so you can practice your times tables from 10 to 20?*

```
120 FOR I=10 TO 20
```

RUN

```
NUMBER? 2
 2  *  10  = ? 20
GREAT!!
 2  *  11  = ? 22
GREAT!!
 2  *  12  = ?
```

2. *If you want to use only the even numbers between 10 and 20, what change would you make?*

```
120 FOR I=10 TO 20 STEP 2
```

RUN

```
NUMBER? 3
 3  *  10  = ? 30
GREAT!!
 3  *  12  = ? 36
GREAT!!
 3  *  14  = ?
```

3. *Try changing the program so it asks you the tables in reverse order, 20 to 10.*

```
120 FOR I=20 TO 10 STEP -1
```

RUN

```
NUMBER? 4
```

```
 4  *  20  = ? 80
GREAT!!
 4  *  19  = ? 76
GREAT!!
 4  *  18  = ?
```

## *PARENT NOTES*

1. This is a very simple example of a math drill program. Encourage your child to personalize the program by changing the responses in Lines 160 and 180.
2. Line 150 is an IF . . . THEN statement. IF M is equal to N * I, THEN the program executes Line 180 next. If M is not equal to N * I, the program executes Line 160. Although this statement is a powerful programming tool, it requires a certain level of maturity. If your child finds this confusing, simply tell what this statement does and eliminate any elaborate explanations.
3. This program can be modified for an addition drill as follows:
   130 PRINT N;" + ";I;" = ";
   150 IF M=N+I THEN 180

# STARS

Seeing stars? Use your computer to print out a universe of stars!

## PROGRAM

```
100 FOR I=1 TO 10
110 LET X=INT(RND(1)*30+1)
120 PRINT TAB(X);"*"
130 NEXT I
```

## RUN

```
                  *
     *
                  *
                          *
                       *
                          *
*
                            *
    *
    *
```

## *LET'S EXPLORE*

1. *This universe has 10 stars. Can you change the program so you can see only 5 stars?*

```
100 FOR I=1 TO 5
```

```
                                   *
        *
                                   *
                                               *
                                          *
```

2. *You don't have to print just stars. Try changing the program so it prints 0's.*

```
120 PRINT TAB(X);"O"
```

RUN

```
                                   O
        O
                                   O
                                               O
                                          O
```

3. *Now, if you wanted to show a fleet of 5 little spaceships that look like ^, how would you change the program?*

```
120 PRINT TAB(X);"^"
```

RUN

```
                                   ^
        ^
                                   ^
                                               ^
                                          ^
```

4. *Think of some other figures or letters you might want to print out and try changing the program.*

## *PARENT NOTES*

1. Line 110 sets X equal to a random number from 1 to 30. This number is then used in Line 120 to space across the page so the * is printed between columns 1 and 30.
2. The equation INT (RND(1) * 30+1) uses two internal functions, the RND (random) function and the INT (integer) function. The RND function gives a random number from 0 to .99 (i.e., .9, .75). The INT function cuts off the fraction part of a decimal (i.e., INT (3.1414)=3).
3. In order to change the range of possible values, replace the number 30 in Line 110 with the biggest number you want. For example, to get a number from 1 to 10, Line 110 should be:
   110 LET X=INT (RND(1) * 10+1)
4. Let your child change the number used in the equation, but don't try to explain how these functions work, unless he/she is ready for that conceptual level.
5. Line 120 uses an internal function TAB. It works just like the TAB key on your typewriter. It tells the computer to move a specific number of spaces across the line and then print. WARNING ATARI OWNERS: The Atari does not have a TAB function. Therefore, this program cannot be used on an Atari.

# SHOOTING GALLERY

Here is a shooting-gallery game you can use on your computer. To aim, type in a 1, 2, or 3. The computer tells you if you hit the target or missed. If you score more than 2 hits in 5 tries, you've done very well!

## PROGRAM

```
100 LET M=0
110 FOR I=1 TO 5
120 PRINT "YOUR SHOT";
130 INPUT N
140 LET R=INT(RND(1)*3+1)
150 IF R=N THEN 180
160 PRINT "BLAM!. . .YOU MISSED. . ."
170 GOTO 200
180 PRINT "BANG!. . .IT'S A HIT!!!"
190 LET M=M+1
200 NEXT I
210 PRINT "YOU HIT ";M;" IN 5 TRIES"
```

## RUN

```
YOUR SHOT? 2
BANG!. . .IT'S A HIT!!!
YOUR SHOT? 3
BLAM!. . .YOU MISSED. . .
YOUR SHOT? 1
BLAM!. . .YOU MISSED. . .
YOUR SHOT? 2
BLAM!. . .YOU MISSED. . .
YOUR SHOT? 1
BLAM!. . .YOU MISSED. . .
YOU HIT  1  IN 5 TRIES
```

## LET'S EXPLORE

1. *Can you change the program so it prints "AAGGHH! YOU GOT ME!" if you get a hit?*

```
180 PRINT "AAGGHH!  YOU GOT ME!"
```

RUN

```
YOUR SHOT? 2
AAGGHH!  YOU GOT ME!
YOUR SHOT? 3
BLAM!. . .YOU MISSED. . .
YOUR SHOT?
.
.
.
```

2. *Change the program to give you 100 points for every hit.*

```
190 LET M=M+100
210 PRINT "YOU SCORED ";M
```

RUN

```
YOUR SHOT? 2
AAGGHH!  YOU GOT ME!
YOUR SHOT? 3
BLAM!. . .YOU MISSED. . .
YOUR SHOT? 1
BLAM!. . .YOU MISSED. . .
YOUR SHOT? 2
BLAM!. . .YOU MISSED. . .
YOUR SHOT? 1
BLAM!. . .YOU MISSED. . .
YOU SCORED  100
```

3. *If you want to get 8 shots each time you play the game, what change must you make?*

```
110 FOR I=1 TO 8
```

RUN

```
YOUR SHOT? 2
AAGGHH!  YOU GOT ME!
YOUR SHOT? 1
AAGGHH!  YOU GOT ME!
YOUR SHOT? 3
BLAM!. . .YOU MISSED. . .
YOUR SHOT? 2
BLAM!. . .YOU MISSED. . .
YOUR SHOT? 1
BLAM!. . .YOU MISSED. . .
YOUR SHOT? 3
AAGGHH!  YOU GOT ME!
YOUR SHOT? 3
BLAM!. . .YOU MISSED. . .
YOUR SHOT? 1
BLAM!. . .YOU MISSED. . .
YOU SCORED  300
```

## *PARENT NOTES*

1. This is a very simple computer game. Line 140 sets R to either 1, 2, or 3. If the number typed in is equal to R, it is a hit. Otherwise it is a miss. Try making up other games with your child, such as shooting at spaceships or submarines, by changing the PRINT statements.

# APPENDIX

RANDOM-NUMBER FUNCTION (RND) The format for this function varies. The Apple, HP-200, Atari, Osborn, and IBM PC use RND (1). The TRS-80 uses RND (0) and the TI uses RND. The Osborn and IBM PC computers require the statement RANDOMIZE in the beginning of the program in order to get a different series of random numbers each time the program is run.

IBM BASICA, Osborn CBASIC, BASIC-Plus, and Altair Extended Basic These versions of BASIC allow string arrays. The programs in this text use standard BASIC, which does not have string arrays. In order to run these programs, leave out the DIM statements.

TI-BASIC Does not use DIM statements with string variables. In order to run the programs in this text, simply eliminate the DIM statement in each program.

Radio Shack TRS-80 Color BASIC Does not use the word LET in assignment statements. Therefore, leave this word out when entering these statements. For example:

Instead of: LET A=B+1
Use: A=B+1

HP-2000 BASIC Requires the statement END as the last statement in every program. Just use a line number larger than any in your program and use the statement END. For example:

200 END

# INDEX